How Absorbent Are Your Shocks?

Everyday Resiliency Tools

Marilyn R. Orr

WESTBOW
PRESS
A DIVISION OF THOMAS NELSON

Cover photo by Bill Orr. For more information, please review his website www.billyorr.com.

WestBow Press books may be ordered through booksellers or by contacting:

WestBow Press
A Division of Thomas Nelson
1663 Liberty Drive
Bloomington, IN 47403
www.westbowpress.com
1-(866) 928-1240

Because of the dynamic nature of the Internet, any web addresses or links contained in this book may have changed since publication and may no longer be valid. The views expressed in this work are solely those of the author and do not necessarily reflect the views of the publisher, and the publisher hereby disclaims any responsibility for them.

Any people depicted in stock imagery provided by Thinkstock are models, and such images are being used for illustrative purposes only.

Certain stock imagery © Thinkstock.

ISBN: 978-1-4497-5515-7 (sc)
ISBN: 978-1-4497-5516-4 (hc)
ISBN: 978-1-4497-5517-1 (e)

Library of Congress Control Number: 2012910194

Printed in the United States of America

WestBow Press rev. date: 06/22/2012

Contents

Acknowledgments

So many people have encouraged me, believed in me, and shared their lives with me in ways that added to my own ability to live life well. Thank you to my friends, my business colleagues, my clients, past and present, and my family. This may sound cliché, but as you get to know me, you will know that I truly let people impact me.

My dad is a living, breathing example of making the most out of life. Thanks, Dad. I also couldn't have asked for more loving, fun, and brilliant brothers. My early skills in resiliency came from surviving a childhood growing up with two big brothers!

My two sons are amazing examples of young men who are making a difference in the world around them. Caleb and Andrew, you both inspire me with your strong values and your passions.

My faith community is made up of so many amazing people. Living extremely authentically with each other has supported my ability to be resilient and has inspired me as I watch these dear friends live out their lives. It has been and is a place where it is safe both to give and to need.

There are many coaches in my life. I have called on many of you to hold me accountable on this project. Accountability without judgment really works! Thank you, coaches!

My colleagues at Vision Coaching Inc. are the most supportive, funny, and warm hearted individuals you could ever hope to work with. So grateful to have such meaningful work with all of you and share our vision: *"a world that values and is transformed by creative, resilient and compassionate leadership."*1

---

1   http://visioncoachinginc.com/leadership.html Accessed May 24, 2012

Without my amazing clients, I would have little to say. Often in the very creative space of coaching someone, brilliant ideas flow. When I know where an idea has come from, and it wasn't from me, I have given credit. However, much of my inspiration has come from my brilliant clients.

Thanks to my friends and clients in Artesia, New Mexico. You have believed in me, welcomed me, given me space to write, celebrated my victories, and grieved with me over the span of many years. Know that you hold a special place in my heart!

Many, many years ago, I read a book called *Love is a Choice* by Dr. Robert Hemfelt, Dr. Frank Minirth, and Dr. Paul Meier. They discuss the concept of "love tanks." I suspect this concept was the seed idea for the model I am presenting here of our energy tanks. Thank you to all of these authors and to Thomas Nelson Publishers for writing and publishing many great books, including *Love Is a Choice*!

God has brought a huge gift into my life recently. Bill is my sweetie, my lover, and my husband. Bill has been so central to my own ongoing wellness. Bill spent thirty years as a car dealer. Using a car analogy is appropriate and very useful. (Our past always has something to give us!) It is absolutely incredible to have a life partner in my sails!

Not only did I gain Bill in my life, but this amazing package also came with two wonderful adult stepchildren. I am so thankful for their acceptance, love, and support. In fact, the majority of photos in this book are the work of William Orr IV, my stepson. Both of Bill's children are talented professional photographers. Thanks Alyssa and Billy for loving me.

Forward

By Dave Veale

'I believe that no matter what you have been through in life, you can increase your capacity for your future.'—**Marilyn Orr**

As you will read shortly, this is one of Marilyn's 'biases'. Knowing Marilyn as a friend, coach, confidant and business partner for over a decade, I believe this to be her mantra. It is a deeply held belief that has guided her on her journey as well as a belief she breathes into those who are lucky to know her and/or work with her.

I cannot think of a person more qualified to educate others on how to build resiliency. I say this because of Marilyn's unique perspective—her ability to take many of life's hardest blows and bounce back stronger that before. I have always been very curious about her capacity to bounce back and marveled at her ability to remain incredibly optimistic and enthusiastic about life. She is one of the strongest people I know.

A wise person, who is also a Master Certified Coach, once encouraged me to take life's challenges head on as 'it will help you become a masterful coach'. In How Absorbent Are Your Shocks, Marilyn—a masterful coach in her own right—not only shares her wisdom on resiliency, she then challenges us to look inward before taking action with our own 'SHOCK Improvement Action Plans'.

So, dear reader, I would like to make a two-part request (I hope you 'accept' this request):

1) You commit to reading this book AND completing each chapter's SHOCK Improvement Action Plan.

2) You share with one person with what you have learned about how incredibly absorbent your shocks are as a result of reading this book!

Marilyn, THANK YOU for having the courage to share your story as well as the fierce discipline to capture your insights in this fabulous book.

Dave Veale, PCC
Founder
Vision Coaching Inc.

Introduction

Poor Shocks

Recently I said good-bye to my Camry. In many ways, it's a great car, but the back shocks are shot. For what the car is worth, we weren't prepared to put the kind of money into it that it would take to fix the shocks and the struts.

With the shocks not working well, the riding experience felt more like riding in a boat on wavy water than driving in a car! Every little bump and every pothole sent the car into serious ricocheting motion. For the first few moments in the car, I found this quite hilarious. Then it got very annoying.

Beyond the obvious annoyance level, this mechanical problem limited the uses of the car. We had to be careful on the curves (i.e., slow down more than we would have needed to in a car with good shocks). We didn't want to take the car any distance. It was okay for getting around town, on the roads we know, and at reasonable speeds.

The same is true in life when our resiliency tools are not working well. We may still be getting through life, but we are living with some impairment. The ride is not as smooth as it could be. It is harder to get back on track after the bumps. Our efficiency and recovery time are reduced, sometimes with significant implications.

I like starting with basic definitions. Here is the entry from the Merriam-Webster Dictionary:

1: the capability of a strained body to recover its size and shape after deformation caused especially by compressive stress

2: an ability to recover from or adjust easily to misfortune or change[2]

So what is it that allows some people to hit small bumps and return to normal so quickly? Why do others get sent reeling from each and every bump on life's road? What is it that allows some people to live through horrific childhoods and go on to be highly productive, successful, and well-adjusted people? How can siblings from the same dysfunctional family grow up to be so different from each other—one sibling off to jail, one a lawyer, and another living with severe addictions? Is it because of personality differences? Is it because of differences in intelligence? How about birth order? Perhaps they were treated differently in the family unit. Maybe a special teacher or neighbor made a difference.

All of those things may indeed play a role and have an impact. However, now as an adult, how much of that can you control or change? Not very much!

This book does not delve in to the whys of varying levels of resiliency. Although I personally find that topic very interesting, it is a much longer road to give you anything useful for today. As a leadership coach, I tend to steer away from the "why" question. I find the question, "What can I do differently that will make a difference?" to be much more helpful. This book is about the really practical things you can do now to increase your resilience. "Personal capacity building" is another term for this that I like a lot.

Even if you are one of those people who others look at as strong and able to just keep going, you also have times when it's really hard to suck it up and keep going. Maybe right now is one of those times in your life.

In general, I am one of those people others see as very resilient. People are often surprised to hear what I am going through or have gone through because I generally keep on functioning at a very productive

---

[2]   http://www.merriam-webster.com/dictionary/resilience, Accessed May 23, 2012.

level. I write this having recently come out of a very hard and long season. There were many times over the past few years when I didn't feel resilient. There were many occasions when what I felt like doing was hibernating in a secluded cabin for three or four months.

Resilience is not about never getting knocked down. It is about having skills and tools to get back up and the ability to get back up quicker.

It is my firm belief that our ability to bounce back can either be inherited (partly genetic, partly learned in our family) or acquired. However, even those people who seem to be naturally resilient are doing things in certain ways that keep them resilient. Resiliency is not about having an easy life; it is about having tools for when life isn't easy. What are the habits resilient people have? How do they think? What have they learned along the way that has made or kept them so resilient?

Interestingly, we could take some very resilient people, and if we taught them some new bad habits, they would really reduce their ability to bounce back. Of course we are not going to do that. I mention this because our ability to be resilient is a direct result of how we think and what we do.

As a leadership and executive coach, it is my job and my pleasure to see the strengths in my clients and help my clients to see them and use them in their lives. Those of you who, like me, did not grow up in a palace have already learned some useful skills for coping with hard stuff and keeping going. My hope in writing this book is simply to add some more tools to your toolbox.

We all have also learned and practiced some behaviors and thought patterns that take away from our ability to move forward in life successfully. Those patterns shut us down and cause us to experience more stress, less happiness, feelings of failure, depression, burnout, etc. Let's live lives that are focused on learning some new habits that bring richness and fullness to our lives!

Over the past few years, I have had many friends tell me that I need to write a book. I think when you are in your own story, living your own life, it doesn't feel like a story you are going to tell others. It just feels like life. However, as a coach and leadership trainer, I believe in the power of stories. We relate to real people so much more than to statistics and facts. We are built for connection. This is some of my story and some stories from people in my life. I hope it encourages your story!

Focus of This Book

I love those books that you just can't put down, don't you? This is not one of those books! It is meant to have little nuggets of information and lots of thought-provoking questions. In fact, each chapter ends with questions for you to ponder and answer, followed by a "SHOCK Improvement Action Plan."

My hope is that you put this book down often to do some thinking, to set a new goal, and to do something for your resilience! I also hope that you pick it back up often to keep working on your capacity building.

There are many wonderful resources out there on resilience from a psychological and therapeutic perspective. I encourage you to read them. A lot of the work on resilience has come out of learning about people's responses to tragedy and crisis. At the end of this book I have included a short list of resources I have found helpful.

As a result of my own career transition from therapist to Certified Executive Coach, my focus here is on everyday resiliency. With that career transition came a move from looking at what is broken to looking at strengths—a move from focusing on the past to proactively creating the future. This book provides a look at resilience and resources from a coach's perspective. It is for you if you are willing to own your own choices and do some work to improve your resilience.

This book examines how to put energy back into your life, where it is leaking out and how to slow or stop the leaks, and how to increase the size of your fuel tank, exploring alternate fuel sources and suggestions for maintenance checks and servicing.

The tools we talk about can help you be more assertive, more stable around conflict, more efficient at processing your own emotions, and more self-aware of your self-talk.

What would a more resilient you look like?

- ✓ You have a more positive outlook on life.
- ✓ You know that you have tools to handle what life may throw at you.
- ✓ You know that you are in charge of your well-being and can do something about it.
- ✓ Not only do you have tools, but you also know how and when to use them.
- ✓ The potholes of life don't scare you as much; you will bounce back from them.
- ✓ Your energy tank may not always be full, but you know how to fill it!

Chapter One

Overview of the Model

The Model

Our minds and bodies are our vehicles to get through life. The condition of our vehicles has an impact on how we can travel through life. Just like a car or truck, you have a fuel tank. It is not a literal place in your body, of course, but it's real. Everything you do in life requires energy. Just like your vehicle, your energy resources are limited. If your vehicle is out of gas, it is not going anywhere. The same is true for you: if you run out of personal resources, you won't get far in life. (And getting towed is not fun!)

Your tank has a limited capacity. Unlike in your vehicle, your fuel gauge is not obvious. We often only know we are low on fuel when we are really low! We are not born with a "fill to here" line or warning light to let us know our tanks are empty.

As discussed in the introduction, the way we respond to bumps in the road seriously enhances or limits our ability to navigate through life. You can still drive with busted shocks, but you sure can't drive as fast, as easily, or on all the normal roads.

I find this vehicle analogy useful for a few reasons, and I have based much of this book on it. First, not all of us drive vehicles, but we have at least been in one and know a little bit about how they work. Second, the analogy highlights the fact that self-care doesn't just happen. Like your vehicle's fuel tank, you actually have to put fuel into your own. We all know what happens if we don't. Third, the analogy is very concrete and fairly visual, which helps us relate to it.

Normal, everyday life is usually like city driving: it requires a fair bit of energy and does not allow us to function at our best. Once in a while, we are fortunate enough to get a stretch of smooth highway driving, which requires less fuel. Let's be realistic, though. Most of life is not highway driving. Much of life is evasive maneuvering—stop-and-go driving—and this seriously drains our energy stores and puts wear and tear on our vehicles.

Tank Capacity

Regardless of the kind of life you have been living lately—fast or slow, relaxed or high stress—your energy gets used up. We have to be able to refill our tanks. This book is about getting better at refueling. It is about strategies for not allowing our tanks to get to empty.

Some of us have small tanks; some of us have larger tanks. Obviously, the bigger your tank, the more capacity you have for fuel. You may have a large capacity but still be living on fumes because of what life has thrown at you lately. Even with a big tank, your capacity may be impaired by having rocks in the tank. Carrying them around really limits your capacity to fill up!

It is my belief, and the premise of this book, that we can:

1. get better at filling up,
2. get the rocks out of our tank,
3. plug some of the leaks in our fuel system,
4. increase the size of our tank,
5. know when the fuel is low before getting to empty,
6. increase the absorbency of our shocks,
7. get better at using other fuel sources, and
8. flush our fluids periodically.

Principles

There are principles behind my approach to resiliency building that need to be discussed before we proceed.

- No matter where you are starting in your resiliency, you can make gains by intentionally working on your skills, thinking patterns, and behavior choices.
- You can always be working on resiliency skills. You can absolutely learn and practice some even when life is going well. If you know how to use the tool well before you need it, using it during a time of crisis or a bump in the road will be so much easier.
- Encouragement works. We get many negative messages every day, and many of them come from inside our heads. It takes a lot of positive to counter the impact of the negative. Many of the questions in this book focus on your successes—the positives.
- You already have strengths you can use to build other strengths. Focusing on and leveraging your strengths are much more effective than trying to fix the weak areas.
- Resiliency tools are often mastered by people who have many opportunities to use them. The people with the best tools are probably not ones who have led easy lives.
- When life has been rough, we can also pick up some ineffective tools. Some of the ways we choose to cope may seem effective in the short term, but in the long run, they will backfire.
- Becoming more self-aware is critical to our wellness and personal capacity. The more self-aware we are, the easier it will be to use tools that move us more quickly and smoothly through the difficult seasons in life.
- Resiliency is going to look different for you than it does for me. What I need to do to be well, to process what's going on, and to move forward is unique to me. Although there are some overarching principles for what is healthy, we are all unique.
- The tools you use now to bounce back may not be the tools you want to use a year from now. As we gain tools, we sometimes gain new preferences. Some tools will be power tools and much more effective than the manual tools.
- Even if it is hard to imagine, by systematically working at it, you can increase your energy for life.

Biases

As a leadership coach, I am trained not to be judgmental and to be very aware of and manage my own biases. I am writing this book, though, with some biases, and I want to be very upfront about them.

1. I believe you are naturally creative and resourceful.
2. I believe that, given the right support and asked the right questions, you can come up with amazing ideas for your own life.
3. I believe that no matter what you have been through in life, you can increase your capacity for your future.

Questions—Chapter One

What potholes have there been in my life in the past two years?

_____

_____

_____

How do I rate my capacity to bounce back based on the most recent situations? (Mark an X)

Very Poor   Excellent

_____

_____

_____

What extra demands on my life are highly likely in the next six months?

_____

_____

_____

Without using the new resources I will find in this book, how do I intend to deal with them?

_____

_____

_____

It is so much easier to see the truth when we apply it to someone else's life. It is sometimes very useful to ask yourself what advice you would give yourself if you were someone else. It can even be very practical to use another name for yourself. (I sometimes use my middle name and write to myself to get a better perspective on something in my life.)

What advice and encouragement would I like to give myself as I start this book?

_____

_____

_____

_____

_____

What is one thing I could stop doing that would help me have more capacity for life's potholes?

_____

_____

What three tools do I already use to bounce back from hard things?

1. _____

2. _____

3. _____

SHOCK IMPROVEMENT ACTION PLAN

Specific chapter goal: _____

How will I do it? (What concrete things can I do to work on this goal?)

   1. _____

   2. _____

   3. _____

Obstacles that could get in my way:

_____

_____

_____

_____

Conditions for success. (What other resources would help me?):

_____

_____

Keeping it going. (How can I ensure continued success?):

_____

_____

_____

Specific benefits. (If I am successful, how will I benefit?):

_____

_____

_____

Chapter Two

Fuel Gauge and Shock Analysis

Broken Gauge

Have you ever owned a vehicle with a busted fuel gauge? I have. It's not fun. You keep putting fuel in but are never quite sure how close to empty you are. There are two times when you can be sure of your fuel level: when you have just filled your tank or unfortunately, when you run out of gas!

Many individuals have described their experiences with crashing to me. So often they were not even aware they had symptoms leading up to the crash. If they were, they sure didn't know how close to burned out they really were. What are the indicators of a low personal fuel level? They include, but are not limited to, the following:

- Being very emotional—cry at the drop of a hat
- Being irritable and grouchy
- Not sleeping well
- Having an upset stomach
- Feeling flat, like nothing is fun anymore

What symptoms do you get when you are running close to empty? Many of these symptoms parallel symptoms of depression. If you have a number of these symptoms, please see a health professional to discuss the possibility that you are currently living with depression. During my career as a therapist, I worked with many individuals who were dealing with depression. It is very common; about one in five of us will have at least one serious bout with depression in our lifetimes.

Fixing Your Gauge

If you have lived for a very long time on close to empty, you may not even know what full feels like for you. If we only have one normal, we don't even need a gauge. As you increase your capacity, your gauge can become your best friend to help you keep from dipping too low again.

When your tank is close to full, you will tend to have more patience and will be less easily stressed. Your emotions will be easier to control, and little things will actually feel little.

In order to talk later about how to fill up your tank, we need to talk about what wellness actually is. There are many models for what human beings consist of and therefore what we need to be well.

We will look briefly at a few versions. However, the biggest takeaway is that you don't need to be functioning at 100 percent in all areas to be doing well overall. In fact, you pretty much have to be superhuman to have all areas functioning perfectly at any given point in time. Let's look at a few groupings.

Early Greek thinking viewed us as consisting of body and soul. The soul was the part that, once missing, meant you were dead. It was more than that, though. "Moreover, the soul is also importantly connected with boldness and courage, especially in battle. Courageous people are said, for instance in Herodotus and Thucydides, to have enduring or strong souls."[3]

There are variations on this. There is the body, soul, and spirit version, the spirit being the eternal part of our being. A common phrase these days is body, mind, and soul/spirit. All of these distinctions are fascinating. What I think is most helpful, though, is breaking down the distinct parts of our lives that make us well or unwell. The categories I find most useful are:

---

[3] "Ancient Theories of Soul," Lorenz, Hendrik, revised April 22, 2009, http:// plato.stanford.edu/entries/ancient-soul/.

- ☐ Social
- ☐ Physical
- ☐ Financial
- ☐ Spiritual
- ☐ Emotional
- ☐ Career
- ☐ Organization
- ☐ Love life
- ☐ Recent losses

These are just my favorites. Please take a moment and think about the categories that make up your wellness. (There is room in the question section at the end of this chapter to do that.)

A great exercise to increase your self-awareness and to get a better reading on your gauge is to give yourself a score using a visual aid. This tool is often called the wheel of life. It is simple but effective. I have filled in a sample here. There is a blank one for you to use in the question section.

In this sample, I picked some of my favorite categories. What will work best for you is your categories, not mine. Organization, for example, may not be on your radar at all. I could fill a few pages here trying to convince you how much organization impacts your life, but I'm not going to. I believe that your quickest path to better resiliency is picking the lowest-hanging fruit in your own life.

I suggest you do this chart periodically and set goals based on your answers.

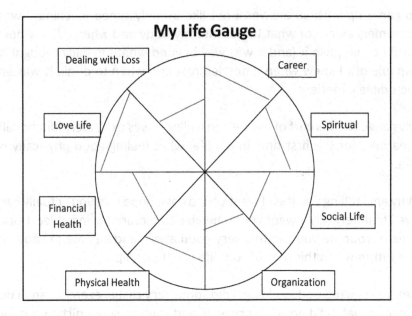

This kind of activity gives me a visual gauge of how I think I am doing in different areas of my life. It also makes me stop and think about the different areas and do an assessment. I think most of us don't do enough of this.

My Story

I want to share an area from my own life where I was able to improve my gauge by being very intentional about improving a specific area of my life. (Remember, if your tank has never been full, it's hard to know where the gauge is reading.)

In the fall of 2006, I decided at the age of forty-one that I wanted to do competitive bodybuilding. In the fall of 2007, I placed second in the regional bodybuilding competition in the province of New Brunswick, Canada.

Recently I had a coach ask me a very good, very perceptive question (which is what coaches are known for). It was very relevant to what she was coaching me on. She asked me, "How did you feel toward your body when you were doing competitive bodybuilding?" It was so easy to come up with an answer. I felt like a finely tuned machine. I was extremely aware of what to put into my body and when. I knew how hard I could push it (and it was way beyond what I initially thought it capable of). I knew when it needed rest and when to drink. It was an incredible experience.

My gauge for this part of my life and wellness was extremely functional! I learned, for the first time in my life, what feeling good physically is like.

Why am I telling you this? I want you to have hope that you actually can live life differently. I want you to be able to picture having at least one area of your life you can feel very good about and be able to know in the future when this part of your life is not up to par.

Before I started bodybuilding, I did some very casual exercise, and I do mean casual. I did not eat very well, and routine was a dirty word for me. If you had told me thirteen months before the competition how incredible I would feel and what I would be able to do with my body, I would have either laughed hysterically at you or started to check on your mental stability!

There is so much capacity in our lives that we are not tapping in to. Each of us, with the right habits, practices, thinking, and resources, is capable of so many incredible things. I learned during that one year of working hard toward the goal of bodybuilding what my body was capable of. The number that blew me away was that I was leg pressing 720 pounds. I felt so capable, so powerful, and so strong.

Have you ever had a season when you aggressively worked on your wellness? People who do that in a sustained and intense fashion actually see results. They are not always immediate, but they are there. Sometimes all of a sudden you realize that something is different.

For months leading up to my competition, my trainer would take pictures of me once a month. Most of the pictures are not very pretty, trust me. (I have included a before photo and a competition photo to prove the point!) Then it felt like all of a sudden, all kinds of changes were visible. I remember the day well when I was completely freaked out by how my thigh felt. I was sitting down and had touched my thigh just to get up. It felt very strange. It was hard and bumpy. This worried me! I went to see my trainer. I told him I thought something was wrong with my legs and that I was concerned. He laughed and informed me that what I was feeling was a muscle without a layer of fat on top of it. Funny! Sometimes the healthy way of feeling is so foreign to us it can be scary. We are so much more comfortable with some of our old, unhealthy habits and their side effects. It can take some getting used to.

Before   **Competition**

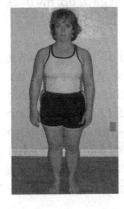

One Year Later

Curve Balls

A couple of years after getting to experience my body in such an incredible state of fitness, I was on a surgery waiting list for my back, hoping I would be able to walk for the rest of my life. As I write this, I live having narrowly escaped back surgery but with a deteriorated disc that is inclined to episodes of sitting on my sciatic nerve. I am grateful that most of the last year has been pain free. I am limited in my exercise to walking and romantic slow dancing.

When was I most resilient? That's the thing—resilience doesn't always show in how together you look to the people around you. I looked pretty "together" as a bodybuilder and businesswoman. I may look less together now, but resilience is about using tools, making choices, and focusing my thinking in ways that allow me to deal with what is coming at me and still stay in the game. The game, or the sport, may need to change, but resilience keeps me in it.

Your Story

Perhaps you also feel like you are living with serious issues that limit your capacity to go for it with respect to your own wellness. Please know that if you put some very intentional effort and time into re-fuelling more often and more effectively, you will benefit!

At both extremes with my back, I have had to be intentional about what I could do to improve my wellness. Believe me, if I just gave up, my back would be much worse!

I tend to be a glass-half-full kind of person. Instead of looking at what I can't do and what all the barriers are, I like to look at what I can do. I also like to pat myself on the back for the good choices I have been making instead of beating myself up about what I did not do (more on this later). With this chapter, my challenge to you—should you choose to accept it—is for you to take some time to reflect. Figure out what categories of your life are most important for your shock absorbency. Be honest with yourself, and start setting some goals to bring up the areas that are putting you at risk.

Questions—Chapter Two

Where would you estimate your fuel level at right now? (Place an "X")

Empty _____ Full

What are the indicators when my fuel is at its lowest?

_____

_____

_____

When my fuel level is at its fullest, what do I notice in my life?

_____

_____

_____

When was the last time my tank was close to full?

_____

_____

If I really believed that I could get my tank full, what would I do differently?

_____

_____

_____

What categories do I think of my wellness in?

_____ _____

_____ _____

_____ _____

_____ _____

_____ _____

My Life Gauge Exercise

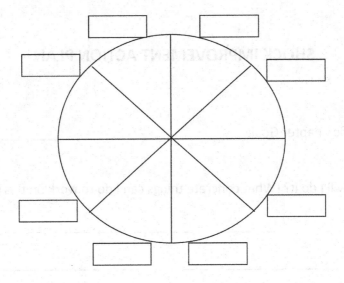

Directions:

The eight sections in the My Life Gauge represent balance. Regarding the center of the wheel as zero and the outer edge as ten, rank your level of satisfaction with each life area by drawing a straight or curved line to create a new outer edge.

SHOCK IMPROVEMENT ACTION PLAN

Specific Chapter Goal: _____

How will I do it? (What concrete things can I do to work on this goal?)

1. _____

2. _____

3. _____

Obstacles that could get in my way:

_____

_____

_____

_____

Conditions for success. (What other resources would help me?):

_____

_____

Keeping it going. (How can I ensure continued success?):

_____

_____

_____

Specific Benefits. (If I am successful, how will I benefit?):

_____

_____

Chapter Three

A Fill-Up

No Right Way

Everyone is different. I like to fill my tank up when I get gas in my car. My husband often puts in a certain dollar amount. My son puts in whatever he can at the time—it might be $5 or $20. There is no right or wrong here; all of these approaches keep your car going. Sometimes what's in or not in our wallets dictates how much fuel we can put in our tanks.

There are times, though, when it's appropriate to fill the tank all the way up. When you are about to go on a long trip, it is useful to fill the tank up. You likely don't want to have to stop often to put more gas in. You also may not have as many opportunities to fill up.

Likewise, there are times in our lives when we will need more fuel and when it may be harder to stop to fill up. Sometimes having the energy to stop for fuel is hard to come by. Heading in to a high-stress time will take much less of a toll if you can go into it strategically. We strategize for so many things; heading in to high-stress times with an effective strategy is one of the most important ways for us to plan personally.

One of my sons has lived for most of his life with fairly serious asthma. He always has a two-stage strategy for dealing with his asthma. Stage one is for normal life. Stage two is if any threat arises. For example, if he catches a cold or is going to be exposed to an allergen, like cats, then stage two applies. It kicks in right away and stays in effect for a number of weeks following the threat.

Strategies

There are two parts to an effective strategy for high-stress times as well. To go the distance during high-stress times, it is extremely helpful to fill up before the high-stress time starts. This is the first phase. Obviously it is not always possible to know when an extremely demanding time is going to hit. However, there are many times when we can reasonably expect that our stress level is going to be high. One quick look at your calendar will give you a starting list: the holidays, specific relatives visiting, an upcoming intense workload, a difficult conversation you need to have, school starting for your children, upcoming medical tests, etc. Being intentional about filling up your tank before a high-demand season gives you more resources to get through it.

The second part of the strategy is to have a plan ahead of time for ways to refuel during the high-stress time. One really helpful technique is to put your refueling times into your calendar. Hoping we will be able to take time out for an activity that keeps us sane is usually not effective. One of the things that makes high-stress times stressful is that there are demands that threaten our healthy boundaries, like deadlines that require longer hours, relatives who will gladly tell us how to do our lives better, and people whose needs blur their ability to think about our needs.

Just like on a road trip, I have to refuel more often during high-stress time. At home I can usually get five or six days out of a tank of gas. On the way to somewhere, I need to refuel partway through the day. It's the same thing in life. I will be burning personal fuel at a different rate during high-stress times.

How can you take time during high-stress times to stop and care for yourself? It definitely changes. It often has to become high-impact intervention. This is a time for supreme grade fuel! I know I can recharge myself by watching a good movie. This, however, is not my most-effective tool. If I was really stressed, I would probably need to watch a few movies, eat popcorn and significant quantities of dark chocolate. Likely if I am very stressed, I do not have time for even the first movie.

If I have a lot of emotional stress happening, my best-quality tool is to do some journaling. Journaling lets me get at the facts, thoughts, and feelings very effectively. I get clarity and depending on what's going on, a good cry. Since I have practiced using this tool for years, it is a power tool now for me. I can quickly get to an effective place with it. Since I have practiced stopping and being honest with myself, I can do that well too when I stop. I schedule "grieving time" in my calendar when I need to do this.

Where Are Your Gas Stations?

What are your power tools for recharging? At the end of this chapter, you will find forms for creating your own high-stress preparation plan and a stress maintenance plan. Why go to the work of completing the forms? Lots of research shows that when we interact more with our ideas and turn them in to concrete steps and goals, we are much more likely to actually incorporate them into our lives.

When I take time to think and plan, I also come up with other ideas that will help me that I hadn't thought of. Maybe there is someone who can support me during this time in really specific ways. Perhaps someone owes you supper and that would be a help.

There are other times when we need a full tank going in to a situation. Preparing to stop an unhealthy habit, such as smoking, or redefining an unhealthy relationship are both times when we will need a full tank. The ongoing success of our new goals depends largely on having adequate resources to make the change.

Do you have a change you would like to make? Who will be really supportive of that change? How can he or she specifically support you while you establish your new habits or boundaries?

Fuel Quality

Not all fuels are equal. Premium fuel (octane rating of ninety to ninety-two) is generally thought to be better for your vehicle, give better mileage, etc. Interestingly, that might not be the case. What your vehicle was made to work best with determines which is really best. Putting too high a level of octane for your vehicle can result in a number of serious problems.

So what's the parallel? There are premium ways for you to refuel your own energy supply. What may be the highest-quality fuel for your best friend may be the wrong fuel for you. What is it that works best for you?

My premium activities include quality time with a best friend, which, for me, means some fun and some heart-to-heart talking. Another premium item for me would be cooking a really delicious meal with my hubby and eating in a nice, relaxed atmosphere.

Not all fuelling needs to be with premium. I simply need to be aware of what energizes me and be intentional, and sometimes systematic, about making those fuel stops. If I can get enough lower-grade fuel in, I can still go some distance on that fuel.

Fuel additives can give you more efficiency. What are the things that supercharge your energizers? It is different for each of us. Since I am such an extreme extrovert, time at a party with good friends—especially if it includes really authentic conversation—really charges me. In fact, I am usually so charged after a situation like this that it takes me hours to unwind so I can go to sleep.

If you are an introvert, you probably don't understand that last paragraph or at least, you cannot relate. The more extreme the introversion, the more you will need time either alone or with the closest of friends. What I just described as really recharging me would likely be exhausting for you.

Stretches with No Stations

I love long-distance driving. I also enjoy the thrill of seeing how far I can get on a tank of gas. For those of you who are familiar with the east coast of Canada, I have gone from Edmundston, New Brunswick, to Ottawa, Ontario, on a tank of gas. This was mostly a fun challenge.

The part that was not fun was getting closer and closer to empty and not finding a gas station nearby. It was not fun at all, in fact!

There are many times in life when a stretch happens that prevents us from our normal energizing activities and routines. We cannot always predict that these stretches are coming. Never getting too low is wise. If we are always working at intentionally doing activities that are life-giving, we can make it through those stretches so much better.

There Is a Station Nearby

The need to be affirmed by others if very real. For many people, it is life-giving. However, unless you are a young child, it is not socially acceptable to go around simply asking to be affirmed. There are some adults who are very good at gracefully asking for affirmation. This is not always easy, achievable, or even wise, though.

Affirmation or encouragement is a vital source of energy. Meeting people's need for affirmation is something I love to do. Some of the needs in our lives that go unmet do so in part because we have tried to convince ourselves that the need is not legitimate. The need to be affirmed is one of those needs many adults try to talk themselves out of.

I think how we get affirmed changes as we become adults. I do not think, though, that our need to be affirmed goes away. In my opinion, we are built to need positive feedback. It is how we function at our best.

Sometimes we find subtle ways of asking for positive feedback, and within limits, that can be fine. However, ultimately we cannot control the behaviors of others. I also don't want to have my real needs to be totally at the discretion of other people.

Depending on your personality, your upbringing, the health of your key relationships, and many other factors, your conscious need for affirmation will vary greatly. Some of you, like me, realize how powerful positive feedback, affirmation, and being celebrated are in your life.

The good news is that self-affirmation can be very effective! Now if you are picturing yourself giving yourself a big hug, don't despair. This goes way beyond that. (Not that there is anything wrong with hugging yourself!)

Not that long ago, I was rear-ended by another vehicle on the top of a bridge undergoing construction. The other driver, a young man, said his foot slipped and he missed the brake. Although that may have been the case, I think it was likely that he was distracted or was even on his phone. I will never know.

What is relevant from this story is that I had choices to make about how to interact with this young man. I chose to treat him with kindness and dignity. By the time we each went our own ways, he was thanking me for being so understanding and kind.

I made another choice after leaving that encounter. I chose to take notice of how I handled a stressful situation and give myself some positive feedback. It went something like this (a rare look inside my head): "Marilyn, way to go! You were very kind to that guy. He was really traumatized by having his first accident. It was clearly his fault, but you chose to think about what he needed also. You still got all the information you needed, but you left him feeling so much better. I like how you handled that!"

I want to encourage you to practice affirming yourself. It really is a power tool that you can always have with you. It is a great way of refueling no matter where you are. It requires reframing how we often look at situations. It will force you to look for the positive, a very good habit indeed!

Questions—Chapter Three

What are the top five things I can do that will put significant fuel in my tank?

1. _____

2. _____

3. _____

4. _____

5. _____

Which of these are premium tools for me? (Effective and accessible.)

_____

_____

The last time it felt like my tank was full, what are some of the things I was doing that helped to energize me?

_____

_____

_____

_____

What is something you have done in the last few days that you can affirm yourself for? (It can be big or small, it doesn't matter.)

_____

_____

_____

_____

SHOCK IMPROVEMENT ACTION PLAN

Specific Chapter Goal: _____

How will I do it? (What concrete things can I do to work on this goal?)

1. _____

2. _____

3. _____

Obstacles that could get in my way:

_____

_____

_____

_____

Conditions for success. (What other resources would help me?):

_____

_____

Keeping it going. (How can I ensure continued success?):

_____

_____

_____

Specific Benefits. (If I am successful, how will I benefit?):

_____

_____

Chapter Four

Leaky Tank and Other Fuel Losses

Where's the Fuel Going?

The first time I drove down to see Bill (we started off in a long-distance relationship), I filled up the tank a couple times each way. It was about a nine-hour drive, so I didn't think much of it. Just a couple of weeks after that trip, my mechanic informed me that my gas tank had holes in the top and I should not fill the tank more than halfway until we could get the tank replaced. The next time I drove to Bill's, I did it on one tank of gas. When I did it the first time, I had nothing with which to compare it.

I had a great but very intense coaching/sharing session with my business partner this past year. He is one of my biggest fans and knows me very well. He gave me some tough feedback. He shared some insights about how I live my life. As coaches, we don't take doing that lightly. There were some "aha" moments for me—painful ones, actually. We sat in tears together for a few minutes.

He has noticed a trend in my life. First I have some times of incredible heights where I am firing on all cylinders and bringing incredible energy to my relationships and work. I have the world at my feet. Then I experience a cycle of lows where I am not running well—times when I am not open to tough feedback because I already feel maxed. In those lowest times, I make choices to put the wrong fuel in my tank, complicating things further.

I had an "aha" moment when I realized that I am not locked in to any relationships where someone has access to cut out the bottom of my tank or willingly siphon off large amounts of fuel. Those things can happen to anyone at any time, but sometimes we are in relationships where that happens on a regular or predictable basis.

Siphoning

Let's start by talking about this common way of losing fuel. We have all experienced people in our lives who steal our energy from us. You know what I mean. I'm talking about those people who, even if it was a short visit, leave you feeling exhausted and drained. What is that all about, and what can you do about it?

These individuals come in all kinds of packages. Part of what makes certain people draining to us is a reflection on something about us; it doesn't just reflect on the other person. The same person may be refreshing for you and draining for me or vice versa. Personality, history, etc., all play a part in how we are impacted by each other. However, there are some people who most people experience as draining. That's our focus here.

To generalize, people who are commonly experienced as draining are consciously or subconsciously trying to get their energy from others. In addition to their fuel tanks being low, they are usually not sure how to fill their tanks on their own. What they are good at is finding people who have fuel and especially finding people who will give their fuel away. This is commonly talked about using "boundary" language.

Sadly, even the fuel they manage to take from us does not last long in their tanks. Part of why they are constantly in need of fuel from others is that their tanks leak and have limited capacity. What I find to be a common belief in these people (and we can all have times when we are this person) is that they are not capable of filling their own tanks. They have a self-limiting belief that they need what you have. They need your cheerfulness, they need your peace, they need your sympathy, etc.

In the previous chapter, we talked about self-fueling techniques. The people who regularly take fuel from others do not have these skills down pat yet. So what can you do about the people you feel drained by? There are a number of options.

1. Spend less time with them. (This can be easier said than done, but sometimes we just need to give ourselves permission.)
2. Plan ahead on how you will set boundaries with this person. One simple strategy is to not answer requests at the time but give yourself permission to tell the other person that you need to think about it and will get back to him or her.
3. Find ways to spend time with the person that are less draining. For example, if the person always wants to tell you about his or her latest crisis, aches, and pains, plan for time together around a fun activity.

My Thinking Is Leaky

One of the ways our tanks spring a leak is through our thinking. How we see the world and ourselves makes a huge difference.

Whether we are truly victims or not is an important factor in our lives. However, how we view ourselves may have more to do with our resilience.

There is a continuum here on our thinking:

I'm a victim   I was victimized, but it   Nothing happened
                   doesn't define me

I recently had the honor of getting to hear Theo Fleury, former NHL all-star, speak. He has a wonderful book out about his own journey. He truly did live life victimized. His bestseller is entitled *Playing With Fire*. He put it well. His defines his own journey as going from

Victim ⟶ Survivor ⟶ Victor ⟶ Advocate

What a great illustration of how his thinking has changed as he has healed.

The Conflict Drain

Conflict in relationships is one big fuel drain! Working with people who are not able to relate well is very stressful. Not having good skills for having difficult conversations can add additional layers to the stress.

Some of you who are reading this book get sick to your stomach at the thought of upcoming conflict. You lose sleep, and you suffer from numerous physical reactions to the prospect of having a difficult conversation. First of all, you definitely are not alone. I really would love for you not to live your life in that zone any more.

From the work I have done with my clients over the years in this area, there are two big things you can work on to reduce the amount of angst that this brings to you. The first is some additional communication skills around conflict. I will give you some examples and suggestions in this chapter. The second is to pay close attention to your self-talk. It is astounding the things we say to ourselves and the impact it has on us. This is such a huge topic that it gets its own chapter, "Talking Cars."

I think the kind of conflict many of us fear the most is the kind where someone else is raging at us. For some of you, this happens on a frequent basis. Please, talk to someone to help you find a way through that situation. The majority of conflict that happens does not take this extreme form. It is milder, and tools to get ready for it and process it after are very useful.

Depending on your comfort and skill level with communicating about uncomfortable things, you will define a conversation as conflict someone else might call a lively debate. The more comfortable we get with communication, the less we end up putting in this category.

Unfiltered Fuel

Learning to filter the advice from others and figure out what will work best for us is critical. What do you think of using secondhand, unfiltered fuel? I put most advice into this category. It might have worked great for the person who is giving me the advice or be an idea that fit well for them. However, since I am not them, since my life is different, my brain is different, etc., the advice may not be effective for me.

David Rock, in his book *Quiet Leadership*, also has some important things to say about giving advice to others. Hands down, your ideas for you and what will work for you are so much more effective. They are also much easier to sell to yourself because you came up with them. This reduces the resistance you may have in incorporating the ideas.

Practical Tools

These tools and steps are not listed in order. Think of them as items in a store. Pick and choose. However, if conflict is very difficult for you, trying as many of these as possible one at a time may really increase your capacity for difficult conversations.

- ☐ Write out what you would really like to say to the other person before talking to him or her.

- ☐ Use a chair, a stuffed animal, or another human being to practice saying what you need to say.

- ☐ Make a list of the impacts on you from the situation you need to discuss.

- ☐ Describe how you would feel if this issue were resolved.

- ☐ What are parallel situations where you have felt this way before? (Sometimes we feel worse because the situation is triggering old stuff.) Write about this.

- ☐ This is not your first difficult conversation. Write about some things you have done in the past that have helped.

- ☐ Get out some of the emotion, whichever emotion it may be, before having the conversation.

☐ When something has made you angry, write a reactive response as soon as possible. This is *not* one to send. If you are doing this by email, I suggest you do *not* write this in an email. Open up a blank document and write it there.

☐ If you have a hard time sending an assertive message, practice writing more assertively (i.e., honestly) by writing your nice response first. Give it a score out of ten on how assertive or honest it is. Then rewrite your response, aiming for one or two points higher on the scale.

Questions—Chapter Four

What are some regular, ongoing fuel leaks in my life?

_____

_____

Do I have any significantly large fuel leaks right now that are sucking out my energy for everyday life?

_____

_____

What thinking do I have that is draining my energy and limiting my beliefs in myself?

_____

_____

What strengths do I have for having difficult conversations?

_____

_____

Who can I practice difficult conversations with? _____

_____

What changes can and should I make to have a healthier relationship with people that I find draining right now?

Name: _____

Change: _____

_____

Name: _____

Change: _____

_____

Name: _____

Change: _____

_____

On a scale of one to ten, how much does conflict, in general, take out of you (one = easy, ten = very stressful)?

_____

SHOCK IMPROVEMENT ACTION PLAN

Specific Chapter Goal: _____

How will I do it? (What concrete things can I do to work on this goal?)

1. _____

2. _____

3. _____

Obstacles that could get in my way:

_____

_____

_____

_____

Conditions for success. (What other resources would help me?):

_____

_____

Keeping it going. (How can I ensure continued success?):

_____

_____

_____

Specific benefits. (If I am successful, how will I benefit?):

_____

_____

Chapter Five

Rocks in the Tank

Rocks and Frogs

I want you to try something with me for a few minutes. Stand up and put your arms up straight over your head. Then lock your fingers together with your palms facing up. Now, for sixty seconds, push up hard. Then release your hands and slowly bring your arms down to your side.

Feel strange? Your muscles are reacting to a new situation. In high school, I used to take piano lessons. My piano teacher used to have me do this exercise to try to keep my shoulders away from my ears!

We get so used to how things are that sometimes we don't know we had adapted to something that doesn't have to be the norm. Some of us have carried around big rocks in our tank for a long time, and we don't even know they are there or that we don't have to carry them.

What are the rocks? They are things from life that have been difficult—things that we were not able to completely process at the time they happened. In reality we have some big rocks, some mid-size rocks, and tons of pebbles sitting in our tanks.

Some of these rocks are really ugly, heavy, sharp pieces of rock. They frequently cause raw pain. Some of these rocks are precious stones. It might be the un-grieved loss of a loved one. The pain we carry around may be one of the only ways we have to keep that person still feeling real and alive to us.

Each of these rocks takes up space and uses up our capacity for day-to-day life. They take away from our capacity for fuel for everyday living. These rocks include natural loss, illness, abuse, unresolved conflict, unrealized dreams, etc.

This topic reminds me of the old story about how to boil a frog. The theory goes that if you put a frog in a pot of cold water and then gradually turn up the heat underneath it the frog, will not react. It adjusts to the gradual changes and doesn't even realize it is in danger.

Resilience or Rocks?

I think this a good place for us to have the discussion about the difference between therapy and coaching. If I was writing this book from more of a therapy frame of reference, we would likely focus even more on your past and spend time getting deep insights we can apply to your life.

Resilience is about being able to function through life's ups and downs. However, when we pick up rocks along the way, we are actually limiting our capacity for future resilience. Picking up tools along the way is fantastic. Picking up false ways of seeing the world is not helpful.

So many times I have heard people say, "I just want to leave that behind me." There is a lot of value to leaving things behind us. However, the route too often chosen to "leave it behind" is simply ignoring or suppressing the events and the impact of them. This is not an effective strategy. It is not an effective way to leave it behind, nor is it effective for life in general.

Sometimes the best way to leave something behind is to actually digest it better—to process it. I need to spend time with that pain to learn what truths or lies I may have picked up from it. I may also find other treasures when I process something.

There are two main benefits from this approach. First, I can actually lay the events of my past to bed much more effectively. Second, by processing the events, I can learn a lot about myself and find better ways of thinking and relating.

43

One of my all-time favorite books is *Life Lessons* by Elisabeth Kübler-Ross and David Kessler. In the chapter on authenticity, Elisabeth writes about the importance of letting go of defense mechanisms we developed in childhood. It is a very helpful read.

Let's use the example of a young lady who learned to use humor in her family to try to ease the tension between her parents. Sometimes it worked but now, in the workplace, she uses humor whenever a serious discussion needs to happen. What used to be somewhat useful has now become ineffective and harmful.

How many of our everyday behaviors are influenced by our emotions and thinking? It is safe to say, the vast majority. Many of these behavioral choices are influenced by thinking that is so natural to us that we are not even aware of it. Cross-cultural experiences are good at getting at some of the assumptions and subtle ways we think about things.

I believe that how we think about things determines how we feel about things that, in turn, impact the behavioral decisions we make. One of the things that makes coaching effective is its ability to get at our thinking. Most forms of therapy do this as well.

If I was writing this with my old therapy hat on, I would be tempted to lead you to do some serious unpacking of childhood incidents, family patterns, the role you played, birth order, etc. All of those activities can be very useful. I personally have benefited a great deal from going down those paths. However, I am writing this book with my coach hat on. In coaching, we often visit older situations in our lives, but it is a much briefer visit. It is very clearly for the purpose of learning what we need to learn for the present and future.

Conclusions

When things happen to me, I draw conclusions from the information I have using the perspective I have. Our brains constantly need to make sense out of things. Many of these conclusions were drawn during our childhood. They were made using what we knew of the world at the time. They formed the core of how we view ourselves, the world, etc. Those core beliefs can either empower us or limit us.

I am watching my cousin and her husband raise their two wonderful girls. They tell the girls often how beautiful they are and how much they love them and set the stage for them to believe the future is wide open for them. Those little girls are being offered an environment where they can draw conclusions about themselves that are very healthy and empowering.

The vast majority of the world grows up in families with at least some dysfunction. Even if you were one of the lucky few who grew up in a healthy family, other things may have happened to you that have had an impact on how you see yourself. When the conclusions we have come to are self-defeating and self-limiting, then we minimize our capacity for a happy, full, engaged, and vibrant life. We have rocks in our tank that limit our capacity for fullness.

The good news is there are some very practical things you can do to get rid of some rocks and shrink some others. If, in the process, you stumble on some big rocks or find that dismantling a rock is getting difficult, then therapy is a very important process to embrace. In the act of getting rid of rocks in our tank, support will also prove useful.

Grief Thoughts

You wouldn't necessarily think that grief could be a hot topic but there are some very divergent opinions on it. How do we most effectively deal with the losses and traumas we have had?

The gold standard used to be Elisabeth Kübler-Ross's work on the five stages. Her work on grief originally came out of work with the dying. There are many variations now on this work and many opinions. Does grief happen in stages? Is it in a particular order or not? Valid questions. However, what matters is that you allow yourself to feel the different emotions and 'stages' that come with grief and know that it is normal. I have been asked many times if it is "okay" to feel angry as part of grief. Yes. It is both normal and common. Grief is not just sadness.

Your Version

I have ways I personally find effective for grieving and processing. They might work for you, and they might not. What matters is that you find the ways that are effective for you.

I would encourage you not to mistake ignoring something for having gotten over it quickly. Do other people see symptoms in you that suggest to them you have some work to do with a situation or relationship from your past?

Questions—Chapter Five

Who in my life can I be completely authentic with?

_____

_____

_____

How often do I take advantage of the opportunity to be with this person? Is this often enough?

_____

_____

_____

What are some of the significant losses and hardships I have experienced in the past five years?

_____

_____

_____

_____

_____

How well do I rate my own ability to actually grieve or process emotion when something difficult happens on a scale of one to ten (one = poor, ten = excellent)?

_____

Which ones do I think I have grieved at least 90 percent?

_____

_____

Which situations or relationships from the past keep jumping up and biting me when I least expect it?

_____

_____

_____

_____

Which ones did I shelve until later (maybe because life just didn't allow me the "luxury" of grieving thoroughly at the time)?

_____

_____

_____

Of the different rocks I am carrying around, which ones am I willing to do some thinking and feeling about so that I can get rid of them or shrink them?

_____

_____

_____

_____

_____

SHOCK IMPROVEMENT ACTION PLAN

Specific Chapter Goal: _____

How will I do it? (What concrete things can I do to work on this goal?)

1. _____

2. _____

3. _____

Obstacles that could get in my way:

_____

_____

_____

_____

Conditions for success. (What other resources would help me?):

_____

_____

Keeping it going. (How can I ensure continued success?):

_____

_____

_____

Specific benefits. (If I am successful, how will I benefit?):

_____

_____

_____

Chapter Six

Just a Few Bucks

Something's Better than Nothing

Have you ever been almost out of gas and not had the ability to just fill your tank up? Sometimes you can only put a few dollars' worth in even though it would be great to just fill up. Those few dollars allow you to keep driving a bit farther, though. It makes so much sense with our vehicles to put $10 in if that's all we can afford at the time. If our tank is on empty, we get that those $10 will let up keep going.

In life we sometimes don't use that principle. When we can't go for a thirty-minute walk, we don't go for a walk at all. This chapter looks at some of the ways we can work at creating patterns where we can frequently put a little energy into our lives.

You know when you go to fill up and the pump clicks off like it is full but you know it isn't? I had a car that did that all the time. It was so annoying. I'd have to pause, pull the nozzle out a bit more, and start again. Learning how to build resiliency can be like this. It requires confidence that these small steps will make a difference. It requires confidence that I have power to make things happen in my life.

I don't care how accomplished you may appear to be to others; unless you know how to set goals and make things happen in your life, you will not feel confident. Confidence building is a very interesting topic. What makes people confident? What makes them not confident? How can you increase your confidence level?

One simple way to gain confidence is to have some success and do it in ways you can notice. Making our success measurable, visual, and tactile can really make a difference. Often as a coach I can see people's skills and giftings, but they have a hard time recognizing them. Although it's nice that I can see and offer encouragement, it is far more important that we can see for ourselves.

Keep Your Marbles

Many years ago, for a counseling course, I had to develop a behavior-modification technique. I decided to create what was called a token economy, where I created values for something. Here's the idea.

1. Get an empty jar, such as a mason jar, and enough marbles or nice stones to fill it.
2. Start with the jar empty.
3. Set five daily goals. These goals should be a bit of a stretch but feasible.
4. At the end of each day, put a marble or stone in the jar for each of the five you have achieved.
5. Before you begin, set a reward for yourself for once the jar is full.

I have done this during many different seasons of my life when I needed to support myself through some change. It's amazing how quickly new

habits form. Research out of the UK says that for a new habit to get to the point of feeling automatic takes 66 days.[4]

My first five daily goals were as follows:

1. Drink five glasses of water.
2. Eat five fruit and vegetable servings.
3. Do some kind of exercise.
4. Don't eat any junk food.
5. Spend thirty minutes in relaxation.

---

[4]   http://www.ucl.ac.uk/news/news-articles/0908/09080401 Accessed May 23, 2012.

There is no taking marbles out! This is purely a way to reward the good choices you make.

I will never forget something my son Andrew did and said when I was doing this. It was very powerful for me. He was around nine at the time. He picked up the jar.

He looked at it, shook it, and said to me: "Mom, isn't it good to know that you did all those good things for yourself!"

He blew me away. He was so right. It was amazing to be able to see (and hear) evidence of all the great choices I had made for myself. The next words out of his mouth were that he wanted to do a jar for himself. That was also very motivating as a parent!

Limited thinking and learned helplessness can really impair our ability to get a full tank of fuel. However, if we practice frequently putting in just a little fuel, but often, we can start to attack our old thinking. It is a more natural to start making small changes when we have learned to see ourselves as helpless and powerless. We need to slowly chip away at our self-perception.

When we have lived a long time with limited thinking, we can adopt an attitude of not doing anything because we can't do all of it. For example, I can't eat as healthy as I want to eat, so I'm not even going to bother eating healthier at all.

I would like to meet the person who started the idea that self-care was selfish! I don't usually like to lecture, but I have a lot to say to that person!

The only way I can care for anyone around me is out of my energy supply. If I burn myself out, I will not be caring for anyone. Not only that, but if I really run out of fuel, I will actually be placing demands on the people around me.

Creating that new habit, as mentioned, takes just over two months. It is more effective to work on creating a new habit that takes care of the troublesome behavior. For example, I want to drink less coffee. Instead of focusing on the habit I want to stop I focus on creating a new habit, drinking 8 glasses of water per day.

Our old habits have some very deeply ingrained triggers that make them hard to extinguish. I can pretty much guarantee if I am adding in 8 glasses of water I will be drinking less coffee!

Breaks

Mental health breaks come in all shapes and sizes. The important thing is to find out where we can turn to when we are trying to find good breaks. Exercise has been shown to be very effective at removing stress from our body. Not only does exercise do magical things in our physical bodies, but it can also give our minds a real break.

There is some great research right now on how time having fun and enjoying beauty can really impact our brain. This is very good news! Dr. Stuart Brown is pioneering work about play with the National Institute for Play. They are "committed to bringing the unrealized knowledge, practices and benefits of play into public life."[5] I had the pleasure of hearing him speak in Asheville in 2011. He and his work are very inspiring.

Playing may be one of the best things you can do for yourself! Some of you may have to remind yourself how to do that! If there are children in your life, they may be able to help you.

---

[5]   "The National Institute for Play" http://www.nifplay.org/about_us.html. Accessed February 7, 2012.

Questions—Chapter Six

If I was to do a marble jar (or some similar equivalent), what would my first five daily goals be?

1. _____

2. _____

3. _____

4. _____

5. _____

What is the reward I will give myself when the jar gets full?

_____

What were my favorite play activities when I was young?

_____

_____

What are three things that I do *just* for fun? (It may have been a while; that's okay.)

1. _____

2. _____

3. _____

In the next week, what am I willing to for fun? _____

_____

_____

SHOCK IMPROVEMENT ACTION PLAN

Specific Chapter Goal: _____

How will I do it? (What concrete things can I do to work on this goal?)

1. _____

2. _____

3. _____

Obstacles that could get in my way:

_____

_____

_____

_____

Conditions for success. (What other resources would help me?):

_____

_____

_____

Keeping it going. (How can I ensure continued success?):

_____

_____

_____

Specific benefits. (If I am successful, how will I benefit?):

_____

_____

_____

Chapter Seven

Hybrids

Options

Part of resilience is resourcefulness. It is the quality of being able to think up new and different ways to tackle a problem. This seems like a fitting chapter for me to be working on right now. I have set aside the next couple of weeks to work on this book. I told friends I was going to lock myself away somewhere so I could just focus on writing.

Ironically, as I type this, I sit locked in the upstairs of my church. My purse, Blackberry, keys, and food are all locked downstairs. It is early Monday morning on a long weekend. I am grateful for many things right now—a wireless connection, Skype, Facebook, and friends who also are up early.

It was interesting to watch my brain go through the levels of realizing how helpless I felt. No keys. No car. No phone. No money. My first response was, *Oh boy—I am stuck now.* I could have panicked at that point and left for a nearby store. I could have been so distracted by the situation that I got nothing else done. (That did happen for a little while.) Thankfully there was a second round of brainstorming. I was able to get online and Facebook some friends, and they kicked into gear, helping to find someone with a key. (Thanks, friends!)

Sometimes we get stuck only filling up in one particular way. Maybe there are fuel sources you haven't even tried yet—other options that are not as immediately apparent to you.

Getting Resourceful

When I look at resilient people, I think this is something they have in common. They are resourceful. Part of their resourcefulness comes from their attitude. They tend to be more optimistic. Instead of getting immediately stuck at the first obstacle, they assume there are other options, solutions, and resources available. The glass is always half full, and they plan on enjoying what's in it.

What is amazing to me is how interconnected the parts of our being are and how they affect each other. My body, my mind, and my spirit are all connected. Whether for good or bad, what I do in one area impacts the others. If I am mentally or emotionally stressed out, physical activity can literally remove some of the stress from my being. This is very, very good news. If I am in the habit of making good choices for myself, I will have some built-in stress reducers.

This interconnectedness also means there may be fuel sources from other arenas than your normal methods that may really be effective at recharging you.

Perhaps you have relied in the past on thinking your way through problems, but you would really benefit from some deep-breathing relaxation activities. Perhaps you have found relief by taking it out on the punching bag at the gym. You might be amazed at what a few journaling exercises could do for you.

It's easy to get stuck thinking about something the way we always have. It's easy to just keep doing the same things to try and get refreshed. I'm going to list a wide variety of ways people get renewed. The point is for you to think outside your current box and try something new.

Alternate Fuel Choices

Be open to trying new ways of getting energized. Some of them will not work well for you. Some of them may surprise you by how fun, efficient, and life giving they are.

My hubby did not try yoga until around six years ago, and now it is a really key part of his physical and mental wellness toolbox.

What is something that you have been curious about trying but haven't tried yet? What are some things your friends rave about that they love and that energize them?

I recommend asking people in your life periodically for ideas. Here are some ideas, just to get you started:

- ☐ Hike somewhere new. Pack a lunch.
- ☐ Shake up your diet. Try some new foods.
- ☐ Start a new hobby, or revisit an old one.
- ☐ Tackle something you have been afraid of.
- ☐ Try a new exercise class.
- ☐ Start volunteering somewhere, and make a difference.
- ☐ Write and read some daily positive messages.
- ☐ Spend time planning who to encourage each day.
- ☐ Slow down, cook a meal, eat sitting down, enjoy every bite, and take your time.
- ☐ Seek out some comedy at a certain time every day.
- ☐ Wake up to a song that really gets you moving.

I could go on forever. As I have coached people over the years on this topic, they have come up with a huge variety of answers to the question, "What energizes you?"

Timing

Sometimes we can get different efficiency out of the things we do to refuel simply by varying the time of day, the frequency of the activity, and where we do it.

My first degree was in science. One of the things it left me with was the ability to look at things in my life as experiments. In good science, you have a hypothesis about how something may work, but you are always open to the data, really determining if it's true.

Experiment with your options, try new ones, fuel at different times of day, and find out what works best for you at this point in your life!

New Stations

We discussed before ways to get a little energized between fill-ups. The idea of thinking about hybrids is that it opens us up even more possibilities for ways to get reenergized for the next stretch of road. In addition to the ways we have already looked at this idea in this chapter, I want us to take some time to think about the various parts of our lives. Looking at an issue from new angles is one tried and true way of generating more creative ideas. Let's look at a few examples.

Financial. Let's say that my finances are an area of stress. I am not getting energized in this part of my life, and I am definitely losing energy because of the stress of it. What are some possible alternate fuel sources I could turn to that I haven't been using?

Most areas have credit counseling centers. Many of these are nonprofit and charge a very nominal fee to help you get finances in order, reduce debt, and work with creditors for lowered interest rates. That's just one option. For many people, their stress level can go way down when they have this kind of support.

Spiritual. Here's an idea that I have added lately. On many mornings, I am the first one up. On some mornings I am energizing myself with some great songs from YouTube. I just put on my headset and crank some great music. Often the songs are spiritual in nature; other times they are just lively, happy songs. It sets a tone for my day!

Social. Perhaps there is a club that would energize you in a number of ways. Clubs allow for fun and social time on top of whatever the meeting is actually about. Is there a club you could join or start?

Questions—Chapter Seven

What have been your traditional ways of filling your tank?

_____

_____

_____

What are some alternative fuel sources that you are willing to give a try? When will you start?

Item: _____

When: _____

Item: _____

When: _____

Item: _____

When: _____

Are there other sources of fuel you are willing to try sometime? What would help you to do that?

_____

_____

_____

_____

_____

Interview a few people you see as highly resilient. Ask them what they do to recharge. Write about what you learned.

_____

_____

_____

_____

_____

What is something you do that you could change the timing or frequency of to see if it is better done differently?

_____

_____

_____

Remember looking at the different parts of your life in chapter 2? Of the different parts of your life, which ones could use additional charging stations?

_____

_____

_____

_____

SHOCK IMPROVEMENT ACTION PLAN

Specific Chapter Goal: _____

How will I do it? (What concrete things can I do to work on this goal?)

  1. _____

  2. _____

  3. _____

Obstacles that could get in my way:

_____

_____

_____

_____

Conditions for success. (What other resources would help me?):

_____

_____

_____

Keeping it going. (How can I ensure continued success?):

_____

_____

_____

_____

Specific benefits. (If I am successful, how will I benefit?):

_____

_____

_____

_____

Chapter Eight

Undercoating

Protective Barriers

This analogy may be lost on some of you—those of you who live in warmer places! (Yes, I do envy you!) Where I live, it's advisable to get your vehicle undercoated. An undercoating on your car doesn't keep the salt from coming off of the road toward your car. It simply puts a protective barrier between the salt and the metal of the car.

There are a couple of different categories we need to talk about. Some of us come in to adulthood with very poor protection in unhealthy relationships. For a whole host of reasons, we may have picked up beliefs about our worth, our lovability, our ability to set boundaries, and a whole host of "shoulds." One misconception I picked up was that I should always be nice to everyone. We will look at our self talk more in chapter 10. Our self talk and how we think about ourselves go together.

The second category where undercoating may need refreshing is when we have gone through something big—a significant loss of some kind—or a series of difficult things. Where I live, people get their cars undercoated every year. The coating gets worn off by the conditions of the road. Let's look at this second category.

Beating the Odds

Beating the odds can be a good thing, but for some of you, it's more like, "What are the odds that one person can have so much go bad so close together?" I've had those seasons—more than once. What happens is that your normal ability to cope or to bounce back vanishes.

Those of you who are walking through some really big, long-term difficulties or who are experiencing one thing after another will have this experience by now. Someone who loves you and who wants you to be well will talk with you about how you need to "get over this." The idea is that you need to be more positive; you have felt sorry for yourself long enough. Your loved one might say, "Too much of that and you will just get stuck there." (This one reminds me of what we were told as kids: "If you make that face too much, your face will get stuck like that!")

Regaining Your Undercoating

If you have gone through a lot of loss, crisis, and change, the odds are good that you have some processing to do. We can call it lots of different things, and there are lots of different ways to do it. As I mentioned in a previous chapter, just trying to minimize it does not fix it long-term.

We can call it:

- ✓ Having some thinking to do
- ✓ Processing
- ✓ Grief work
- ✓ Paradigm shift time
- ✓ Healing

Once the protective barrier has been worn down, we are more vulnerable to everything around us. Stuff that would not have bothered us before is a big deal now. Our normal ability to put things into perspective is shot. We have been overloaded.

There is a huge difference between wanting to feel like crap to get sympathy and truly having things to deal with. Most people really have things to deal with and simply don't have the tools to do so. Sometimes making ourselves just think positively can be a way of avoiding the work we need to do. We touched on theories on grieving in chapter 5. I want to give you a few more tools here.

Objective measures help a lot when we have gone through a lot. One of the ways our minds help us be resilient is to minimize what we've gone through. This helps us cope. We also use this minimizing skill with other people so they don't see us as complainers or weak.

Here are some of the common things we say to ourselves:

- There are so many people who have it so much worse than me.
- Stop living in the past; get on with life.
- It's not that bad. People deal with this stuff all the time.

You get the idea. There are so many versions of this kind of self-talk, and it is unfortunately reinforced all too often by society. Here are some of my all-time favorite incredibly awful sayings (many with ridiculous sexism built in for added insult):

- Put your big-girl panties on.
- Be a man.
- Stop your whining.
- Don't be such a girl.

Life improves so much when we stop taking in unfiltered advice. There are times when we need a new, more effective filter. One of the things I find so refreshing about using a coaching approach to life is that it minimizes the giving of advice. So many people are quite happy to give us advice to fix our lives with. All too often neither they nor we are filtering this advice!

When I am coaching people who have gone through a lot, it always helps them when we actually make a list of all the things they are dealing with. Sometimes just saying the list out loud to someone else and hearing them acknowledge how much you are dealing with can go a long way.

The second half of this chapter is dedicated to talking about making use of appropriate professionals. I'm a believer in using professional help, having done so numerous times. These ideas do not replace getting appropriate support, but they may help you get started on some recovery. Some of the tools we have already talked about may help, but here are some specifically for those of you with a series of big things.

☐ Make a list of all your significant losses in the past twelve months.
☐ Take a stress-scale inventory. (http://stresstest.net/ offers an option from Behavioral Health Concepts Inc.)
☐ Talk to your doctor about how your body is doing. (Your sleep, stomach, appetite, etc., can all be impacted by numerous crises.)

If this is your life right now, it's time to be aggressive with your wellness! Undercoatings don't just magically reappear when they have been completely worn off.

Internal Coatings

I think of the internal coating as a way I can protect myself from outside events, people, stresses, etc. It is primarily about how I am thinking about myself and the world around me. It is me having the power to set good boundaries and make choices to do what I need to do to be well.

When we are really worn down, this is tough. It's also tough if we never learned how to do this in the first place. One great place to build up these internal self-protection layers is with the right professional. In my experience, the safest professionals in these areas are the ones who have also had to do this development work. They get it, and they don't judge!

External Coatings

Sometimes the support we need is in the form of someone else. There is such a long list of the types of support that we could do a book just on this. However, I am going to focus on the ones I have personally found highly effective in my life and for the people I have worked with.

Having a personal or professional coach is a great way to get regular feedback and support in getting an accurate perspective on relationships and situations in your life. A coach provides a safe place to think things through, test out your perspectives, and hear your thoughts out loud. The International Coach Federation "defines coaching as partnering with clients in a thought-provoking and creative process that inspires them to maximize their personal and professional potential."[6]

Coaches ask thought-provoking questions. They don't have our blind spots. They don't have our fears. They can challenge our thinking, lead us to insights, and support us through our growth. Coaches don't come with preset steps for us to follow to improve our relationships. They come ready to strategize with us. They help us develop custom-built goals and actions based on our wisdom, our limits, and our hopes.

As a leadership/executive coach, clients often ask me to help them prepare for difficult conversations. Those people who are damaging to our wellness come in all parts of life. They can be our coworkers or our family or friends. They can be where we volunteer or on our sports teams. Setting up healthy ways of relating to these people makes a huge difference to our ability to get through life well. Toxic people can really cause the bottom to fall out of our lives in a hurry.

Thicker Undercoating

Some of us—and it was true for me—find ourselves with little to no idea of how to protect ourselves from unhealthy, toxic relationships. Counseling and therapy can play a critical role in getting those barriers in place. Sometimes our thinking needs an overhaul. If you see an unhealthy pattern in a number of your relationships, it is likely time to talk with a mental health professional.

During my early twenties, I was in a relationship with a young woman who lived with serious, chronic mental illness. She had episodes when she was quite violent. I lived in fear. I had no idea how to create a protective layer between us. When I was with her, my only strategy was

---

[6]   http://coachfederation.org/about-icf/overview/ Accessed May 24, 2012

to tell her what she wanted to hear to protect myself in the moment. That ended up fuelling the unhealthy pattern. I was not bouncing back! This relationship took a serious toll on me.

I had pretty much no undercoating. I was extremely vulnerable to what the people around me chose to do. The result of having no protection and having a toxic relationship in my life was almost complete life paralysis. I was afraid to answer the phone. I was afraid to leave my apartment.

However, this relationship started me on my journey to healing and taking an honest look at how I was doing relationships and thinking about myself. I had no idea how to say no to this woman. I had no idea how to keep myself safe. My anxiety level was through the roof.

The crisis that this put me into caused me to do an inventory of my relationships. The pattern was so obvious. I was in rescue mode. Most of my relationships were based on me "helping" the other person. Someone could have written a book on codependency based on my life.

My undercoating started with the assistance of some great self-help books. If you have a difficult time having healthy boundaries with other people, I highly recommend the book *Boundaries: When to Say Yes— When to Say No—To Take Control of Your Life* by Dr. Henry Cloud and Dr. John Townsend. This book is written specifically from a Christian perspective. If that is not your belief set, there is still excellent material in it. If that is your value set, this book may help you with baggage you may have picked up about what healthy boundaries are.

I would have gotten my life back much quicker had I gone for counseling, but it wasn't even an option I considered back then. It would have save me a lot of grief and shortened my journey to healthier relationships. I finally dealt with a lot of the underlying beliefs that had left me so vulnerable to unhealthy people when I was working on my master's in counseling.

PS

Some professionals are open to bartering. You may not have insurance or money for some services, but you may be able to trade something else of value. (In most places, appropriate taxes should still be paid on the market value of these services. I am not suggesting otherwise.)

Questions—Chapter Eight

Who are the people in my life I can count on for some encouragement and/or support?

_____

_____

_____

What are the difficult things I have been dealing with in the past twelve months?

_____

_____

_____

_____

_____

_____

How is this series of hard things showing up in my life and body?

_____

_____

_____

_____

What strengths do I see in myself that have kept me persevering? (Yes, I have persevered; I'm here reading this book!)

_____

_____

_____

What is one way I try to minimize or make light of what I've gone through lately?

_____

_____

What's getting in the way of me spending time with an appropriate professional? What are the barriers?

_____

_____

_____

What are some possible solutions to those barriers?

_____

_____

_____

SHOCK IMPROVEMENT ACTION PLAN

Specific Chapter Goal: _____

How will I do it? (What concrete things can I do to work on this goal?)

1. _____

2. _____

3. _____

Obstacles that could get in my way:

_____

_____

_____

_____

Conditions for success. (What other resources would help me?):

_____

_____

Keeping it going. (How can I ensure continued success?):

_____

_____

_____

Specific Benefits. (If I am successful, how will I benefit?):

_____

_____

_____

Chapter Nine

Maintenance Routines

Every Three Thousand Miles

So you have been working on regularly putting fuel in your tank; fantastic. You have also been getting rid of some of the rocks that have been limiting your capacity. Sweet. You have or are getting a better undercoating.

Every so many miles (or kilometers), it is important to do a flush of your system. In a vehicle, the list includes oil changes, radiator flushes, rotating the tires, etc.

For our vehicles, we think about what kind of oil is needed for different weather conditions. We change our windshield washer fluid as well for significant weather changes. Even different tires are useful if we live in a part of the world that gets sustained cold temperatures.

You can keep running your vehicle without these maintenance procedures, but you will impact safety, fuel economy, engine wear, and ultimately, the life of your vehicle.

Every area of our lives has the potential to get seriously out of alignment. I'm going to use a few of the most common categories for us to talk about ways to get a fresh start.

For many of the more effective flushes in our lives, dedicated time is critical. If you have the luxury of taking yourself on a personal retreat away somewhere, that can be effective. (Many cities have Catholic retreat centers that are phenomenal at providing the right kind of atmosphere for a personal retreat.) Even using a friend's house while he or she is out at work is better, for most of us, than trying to stay home and focus. There are too many distractions.

Relationships

Relationships change and grow over the years. Some relationships that used to be good for us can become unhealthy. It can sneak up on you. Taking time to do a relationship inventory once in a while is a great idea.

☐ Who in your life encourages you and your growth?
☐ Who leads you down paths that are not good for you?
☐ Which of my friends/family are the most positive (in a genuine way)?
☐ Which of my friends/family are consistently very negative?
☐ Who am I always rescuing or trying to fix in some way?
☐ Of my relationships, who can I be most genuine with?
☐ Do I have any toxic relationships?
☐ What kind of relationship is missing?
☐ Who do I want more time with?
☐ Who do I want less time with?

Some relationship changes can simply be casual shifts in how much time is spent with that person. Some of the relationship guck we carry around can be easily cleared up by an honest conversation with the person involved. However, there are many times—either because one or both people lack the conversation skills or because the wound is so painful or complicated—that resolving an issue with the other person is really hard.

I truly believe in trying to have a conversation with the other person when it's both wise and possible. Some unhealthy relationships can really be improved with an honest conversation. (I don't recommend confronting an abuser in your life without excellent, professional support.)

If your inventory reveals a number of unhealthy relationships (like one of mine did years ago), you have some work to do! Earlier I recommended the book *Boundaries*. There is another great resource for evaluating and transforming how we relate, and that is the book *Co-Dependent No More*. It's a classic.

Physical

This is such a large and important area to focus on. It's about our diet, our exercise, and our sleeping. It covers self-care practices, like getting to the dentist and doctor regularly. It includes looking at the unhealthy addictions we have.

Making even small changes in one area can go a long way! In fact, small changes that are sustained are often more effective. However, with the right support and drive, overhauls are possible. I am probably in the minority, but I have found making huge changes all at once can sometimes be easier for me. I went straight from normal, meat-heavy diet to a vegan diet (this is vegetarian but also without dairy or egg). I went from just starting to exercise regularly to competing in bodybuilding. That's how I work.

The bottom line is, keep working on getting healthier.

There are so many professionals in this area. If you are feeling overwhelmed about where to start, adding the support of someone in the wellness field may be just what you need.

My trainer, John, believed in me and my abilities to change when I couldn't yet. The dietician I'm working with now knows so much about helping me eat a balanced vegan diet. They have trained specifically to help people get healthier, and they understand the barriers that get in our way.

Overhauls are fantastic when you can do them. Sign up for a boot camp, train for a marathon, radically change your diet, hire a trainer, engage a dietician, see your doctor for help quitting smoking, etc.

If you are only ready for small changes right now, here are some questions:

☐ If I were to start eating more healthy foods, what foods would I add?

☐ Of all the unhealthy foods I eat, which one am I willing to give up or limit?

☐ What exercise could I add three times per week (even ten minutes helps)?

☐ If I added one more glass of water per day, when would I drink it?

Spiritual

There are so many ways you can attend to your spiritual needs. For some of you, spiritual includes religious disciplines and practices. For some of you it will be more of a focus on mental health practices.

There are so many facilitated retreat options around right now. This can be a very life-giving way to refresh your existence. Spending a weekend with other people who want to grow in similar ways is very powerful.

Another great way to reboot spiritually is to attend a visioning session or take yourself away somewhere and walk yourself through one. Creating vision boards or pictures is very popular right now, and for good reason. There are many resources online to do this, including exercises to help you narrow down what your most important values are.

Here are a couple of good websites (accessed May 24, 2012):

http://christinekane.com/how-to-make-a-vision-board/

http://www.oprah.com/spirit/How-to-Make-a-Vision-Board-Find-Your-Life-Ambition-Martha-Beck

What spiritual practices in your life are the most renewing? What gets you up in the morning? How can you let that have a bigger impact on your life in general? Whose spirituality do you admire?

As usual, there are people who specialize in helping us spiritually. Once again, Catholic retreat centers often have people resources too. Spiritual directors are people trained to help you on your spiritual journey. Not all spiritual directors are Catholic, but they have really led the way in this area (and I am grateful). Music, art, theater, nature, meditation, journaling, dance, massage, primal screaming, photography, humor— the list is endless. What will enrich and refresh you spiritually? When did you feel most spiritually healthy and alive? What were you doing at that time in your life?

Financial

When this area is in bad shape, it is so stressful. So many areas of life can literally be changed by making self-disciplined choices. Although that is definitely a part of achieving and maintaining financial wellness, there are many other factors beyond our control. Breakthroughs come by changing what we can change.

When we get really discouraged in a particular area, we just give up. Giving up compounds the problem in ways that we cannot calculate because we have already given up.

Donuts make such great analogies. If I ate one donut, I could easily say, "Well, I blew it now; I might as well have another one!" The second donut is doing just as much damage to my body as the first one. It counts. It has just as many calories.

We can do the same in our spending. "I'm broke anyway so . . . I'm in debt already so . . . ." The reality is that small changes in spending can add up to big changes in our finances. There are great stories of people on very low incomes who had patterns of saving small amounts of money on a regular basis. As a result, they were able to have a big impact on the lives of other people. Inspiring!

Where do you tend to be most irresponsible with your spending? Even if it's a small amount, what could you do to save a bit of money for the future or a special project or event? It can be as simple as saving your change and not touching it.

Once again, many professionals in this area are happy to help. Getting support to create a realistic budget and living within it greatly reduces stress. There are many practical ways to sort your money to visually know what you have to spend at any point in time. So much of our spending is with a card, and we lose track of what we have and don't have at our disposal. Getting help to be more aware of our financial realities may not be pleasant, but gaining control of our financial situations will have a huge impact on our lives.

Questions—Chapter Nine

What do I want more of in my life?

_____

_____

_____

_____

What do I want less of in my life?

_____

_____

_____

_____

What supports can I include in my life to help me reset an aspect of my life?

_____

_____

_____

Which relationships do I need to encourage?

_____

_____

Which relationships do I need to end or minimize?

_____

_____

If I could get the right supports, my hidden dream would be to . . .

_____

_____

Which area of my life needs the biggest overhaul? (You may refer to the wheel from chapter 2.)

_____

After that overhaul, how would my life be different?

_____

_____

_____

What is it costing me and what will it cost me not to do this overhaul?

_____

_____

_____

_____

SHOCK IMPROVEMENT ACTION PLAN

Specific Chapter Goal: _____

How will I do it? (What concrete things can I do to work on this goal?)

   1. _____

   2. _____

   3. _____

Obstacles that could get in my way:

_____

_____

_____

_____

Conditions for success. (What other resources would help me?):

_____

_____

Keeping it going. (How can I ensure continued success?):

_____

_____

_____

Specific benefits. (If I am successful how will I benefit?):

_____

_____

_____

Chapter Ten

Talking Cars

Advice from Your Vehicle

Some of you are old enough to remember the phase when vehicle manufacturers thought it would be a good idea if cars could talk to us. You know—tell you that you were low on fuel, remind you it was time to get an oil change, etc.

If you are too young to have experienced how annoying that feature was, you can probably get the same feel if we talk about using a GPS device that doesn't have up-to-date maps. One of my favorite incidents with a GPS gone bad was when I was driving through Montreal, Quebec, Canada. (If you have tried to navigate your way through Montreal, you may literally feel this story in your gut.) I was either on Highway 20 or 40 heading to Ottawa. Montreal highways are known for congestion, lack of shoulders on either side of the lanes, fast speeds, and frequent construction. As I was in the middle of concentrating on driving in the middle lane, which seemed the safest, my GPS told me to "turn left now." It wasn't hard to ignore that advice. It was very obvious it was incorrect.

You Are Getting Bombarded

Less obvious are the messages we send to ourselves, often hundreds of times per day. You are probably so used to your own self talk that you don't even notice it! There are multiple themes to our self-talk. Not too many of them are positive and life-giving.

One theme is simply trashing ourselves with messages like, "That was stupid," "OMG, you look so fat," etc. Another theme in our self-talk is comparing ourselves to other people. Our self-talk lines up with our self-limiting beliefs. This internal voice we use so often brings with it very consistent messages about our self-concept.

Are You Visual?

I am very visual, so having a visual illustration of things helps them stick for me. Dale Carnegie programs use a lot of visual tools to help people remember things. It works.

When I was training to be a coach, one of my professors, Marj Busse, gave a great demonstration I will never forget. She stood at the front of the class with this rubber duck on her shoulder. She talked about how we all have these voices talking to us. It's like having a duck sitting on our shoulder most of the time, quacking away. You're trying to talk to someone, and it's quacking. You are doing a presentation at work or school, and it's quacking. Very annoying! "Quack, you aren't prepared enough! Quack, she thinks you are stupid, quack."

It is very hard to concentrate when you have someone talking in your ear about something else. (Yes, I have tried this, on purpose. It is very difficult!) Our goal with this annoying little duck is to shut the duck up! As Marj explained this, she sent her duck flying across the room. It was hilarious but also such a very practical and effective way to think about our negative self-talk.

I probably find this analogy too much fun. (Blame it on my family's twisted sense of humor!) These ducks not only quack incessantly, but they also poop all over us. They can leave us covered. That's pretty visual!

So how do we shut the duck up? (And get it off our shoulder!) In the question section for this chapter, there are some exercises and questions to help you shut your duck up.

DUCK HUNTING SEASON

1. Before we can shut the duck up, it helps to know what it's saying. To do this, simply pay attention to yourself in different kinds of situations. Sometimes the ducks get busy during the night. They are often very noisy if we feel like we have made a mistake or dropped the ball on something.

2. Where did you pick up the hitchhiker? Sometimes it's helpful to know if this duck is an old duck we picked up from someone else. It isn't always, but sometimes knowing this duck is really a new form of Aunt Gertrude, for example, can really reduce the volume very quickly. If I know a critical duck message came from my mom and I am very sick of having her criticism control my life, that insight can help motivate me to stop giving so much power to this duck.

3. Write out replacement messages. Coming up with a new message will require both a logical analysis of the content and some emotional intelligence work. I can logically tell myself that my duck is wrong when it tells me I'm stupid, for example. I can come up with clear examples of things that demonstrate I am smart. That is the logic side to duck hunting.

From the emotional side, I must have another discussion with myself. It's likely the more important side. For example, it might go something like this: "Marilyn, I can prove to you that you are not stupid, but that's not even the point here. You are allowed to make mistakes. People love you just the way you are. It was important in your family to be smart, but it's not the be all and end all. I love your humility and how you own your mistakes. Way to go!"

It is important to own anything true that I need to work on, but beating myself up usually just paralyzes me and is not productive in any way.

4. Practice the rebuttals. Now, since I have long-established habits with the old messages, I will need to literally create new pathways in my brain. Remember, after a couple of months this will be automatic! That's good news.

    At first we will have to catch the ducks quacking. That takes practice. Then we will have to work on having our comeback ready. The more we do this, the shorter the time gets from when we notice the duck quacking to when we can shut it up. At first we might not even realize the duck was quacking until much later. It is helpful to start noticing when the quacking starts. The quicker we can clue in to the mean little thing speaking bad about us, the quicker we can shut it up!

Fowl Prejudice

For the most part, people like to think of themselves as unbiased, unprejudiced, kind people. However, the things we say to ourselves in our self-talk are anything but kind!

Just for a minute, picture someone else following you around all day saying to you the things you quietly say to yourself. Even just saying your self-talk to yourself out loud can be quite shocking!

We wouldn't likely allow someone else to follow us around all day and talk to us the way we let our duck talk! We are letting these little birds get away with some very foul behavior!

It's a great rule of thumb that if you wouldn't want someone else talking to you in the way you talk to yourself, you also should not talk to yourself that way. Here's to shutting up the mean little ducks of the world! What a better place it would be without all those negative, destructive messages.

Farewell

It is my dream that this book has inspired you and challenged you to make choices that have and will increase your resilience. May life's road rise to meet you, may your shocks be ready for the bumps!

Please share your story with others and inspire them. As we live life open to each other we are forever changed by those encounters!

Questions—Chapter Ten

What do my ducks say to me (my self-talk)?

_____

_____

_____

_____

_____

_____

Do I recognize any of these ducks? (Have I internalized someone else's voice [e.g., my mother used to criticize how I was dressed]?)

_____

_____

_____

_____

_____

_____

What are the themes I see in the negative messages I send myself?

_____

_____

_____

For each negative script I have, what is a more positive, accurate message?

Old: _____

New: _____

Old: _____

New: _____

Old: _____

New: _____

Old: _____

New: _____

Old: _____

New: _____

How can I remind myself about the new messages?

_____

_____

_____

SHOCK IMPROVEMENT ACTION PLAN

Specific Chapter Goal: _____

How will I do it? (What concrete things can I do to work on this goal?)

1. _____

2. _____

3. _____

Obstacles that could get in my way:

_____

_____

_____

_____

Conditions for success. (What other resources would help me?):

_____

_____

Keeping it going. (How can I ensure continued success?):

_____

_____

_____

Specific benefits. (If I am successful, how will I benefit?):

_____

_____

_____

Resources

DR. DAN B. ALLENDER, *The Wounded Heart: Hope for Adult Victims of Childhood Sexual Abuse.* (COLORADO SPRINGS, CO: NAVPRESS, 1995).

MELODY BEATTIE, *Co-Dependent No More: How to Stop Controlling Others and Start Caring for Yourself.* (CENTER CITY, MN: HAZEDEN, 1986).

DR. HENRY CLOUD & DR. JOHN TOWNSEND, *Boundaries: When to Say YES, When to Say NO to Take Control of Your Life.* (GRAND RAPIDS, MI: ZONDERVAN, 1992).

THEO FLEURY, *Play*ing With Fire. (TORONTO, ON: HARPERCOLLINS PUBLISHERS, 2010).

DR. ROBERT HEMFELT, DR. FRANK MINIRTH & DR. PAUL MEIER, *Love is a Choice: Recovery for codependent relationships.* (NASHVILLE, TN: THOMAS NELSON PUBLISHERS, 1989).

ALISON HENDREN, PAM RICHARDE & AMY RUPPERT, *365 Coaching Questions.* (COACHING OUT OF THE BOX, 2010).

ELISABETH KUBLER-ROSS & DAVID KESSLER, *Life Lessons.* (NEW YORK, NY: TOUCHSTONE, 2000).

DANIEL H. *PINK, A Whole New Mind: Why Right-Brainers Will Rule the Future.* (NEW YORK, NY: THE BERKLEY PUBLISHING GROUP, 2006).

DAVID ROCK, *Quiet Leadership: Help People Think Better—Don't Tell Them What to Do!* (NEW YORK, NY: HARPERCOLLINS PUBLISHERS, 2006).

DR. SANDRA D. WILSON, *Released From Shame: Moving Beyond the Pain of the Past.* (DOWNERS GROVE, IL: INTER-VARSITY PRESS, 2002).